Ubel Velez: Lawyer

Published by
Twenty-First Century Books
38 South Market Street
Frederick, Maryland 21701

Text Copyright © 1991
Jennifer Bryant

Photographs Copyright © 1991
Pamela Brown

Printed in the United States of America

10 9 8 7 6 5 4 3 2 1

Cover and book design by Terri Martin

Dedicated to all of the working moms
who helped with this project

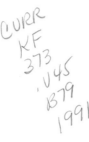

Library of Congress Cataloging in Publication Data

Bryant, Jennifer
Ubel Velez: Lawyer

Summary: Portrays the everyday life of a hard-working Hispanic-American
lawyer who is also a busy mother raising a family.
1. Velez, Ubel—Juvenile literature. 2. Women lawyers—United States
—Biography—Juvenile literature. 3. Working mothers—United States
—Biography—Juvenile literature.
[1. Velez, Ubel. 2. Lawyers. 3. Working mothers.]
I. Brown, Pamela, 1950- ill. II. Title. III. Series: Working Moms.
KF373.V45B79   1991   340'.92—dc20 [B]   90-25322 CIP AC
ISBN 0-941477-52-5

Working Moms: A Portrait of Their Lives

Ubel Velez: Lawyer

Jennifer Bryant
Photographs by Pamela Brown
Photographic Consultant: Bill Adkins

TWENTY-FIRST CENTURY BOOKS
FREDERICK, MARYLAND

"You are listening to radio station WPST, the morning talk of Wilmington, Delaware. Now don't put your head back on that pillow. It's 6:00 A.M. Time to begin another busy day."

Ubel Velez awakens with a start. She turns to look at the alarm clock and blinks in disbelief. But the "morning talk of Wilmington" is right—again. It *is* 6:00 A.M. And it *is* time to begin another busy day.

"Busy" is a good word to describe the day ahead. As she climbs out of bed, Ubel thinks about the many things she has to do today. There are some important cases that need her attention. Ubel Velez is a lawyer. Her job is to give people advice about the laws of our country. There are hundreds of different laws. They are the rules about what we are allowed to do and what we are not allowed to do. They are made to protect the rights and safety of everyone.

Ubel works to make sure that her clients, the people who come to her for help, know what their rights are under the law. She works to make sure that her clients are treated fairly and equally under the law. It's a job with a great deal of responsibility. Many people depend on her work.

But her clients are not the only ones depending on Ubel. She has a family depending on her, too.

Lots of people are depending on Ubel Velez. She's a working mom.

Breakfast is almost ready, but where are Cecilia and Yazbehl? Ubel's husband, Manuel, sighs as he goes to call the girls. "Every morning, it's the same thing," he mutters, mostly to himself. "Just what do they do up there?"

But Ubel smiles and remembers what it was like to be a teenager. How important it was to look good every day!

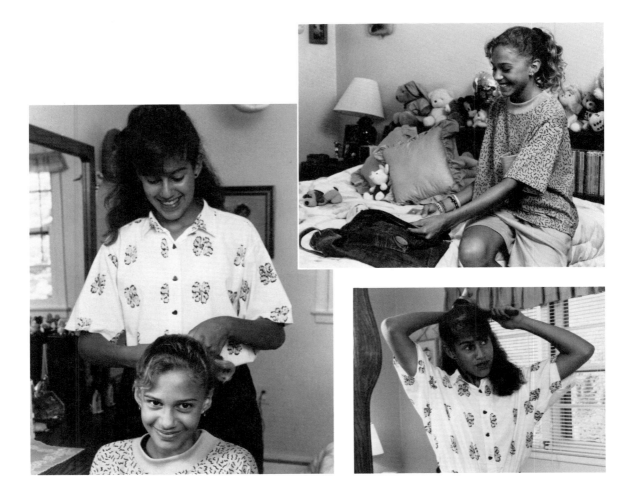

"Breakfast is ready," she hears Manuel say, "and if you two don't hurry up, I'm going to eat the rest of the cornmeal myself!"

That gets them down fast. Cornmeal for breakfast is a family favorite. "Gracias, Mama," Cecilia says. That means "Thanks, Mom" in Spanish. At home, the Velez family speaks in Spanish.

"It reminds us of our Hispanic heritage," says Manuel. "It reminds us of who we are."

The Velez family is proud of its heritage. Ubel and Manuel were born on the island of Puerto Rico. On the northwest coast of Puerto Rico lies the little town of Camuy. There Ubel Velez grew up, with her aunts, uncles, cousins, and grandparents close by.

Her parents both worked. Ubel's mother was a teacher, and her father was a policeman. They worked very hard to give their children the things they could not afford when they were growing up. Most important, her parents thought, was a good education.

"The sky's the limit," Ubel remembers her mother saying. "She would always tell us that: 'the sky's the limit.' She encouraged me to aim high. 'Follow your dreams,' she would say."

"My parents believed that education was the key to the future. They believed that a good education was the way to make dreams come true. They taught me how to set goals for myself, even if those goals were far away. They showed me how to work hard each day, how to get a little bit closer to my dreams each day. It wasn't always easy. But my hard work paid off. I'm grateful to my parents for teaching me the lesson of education and hard work. Now I have to teach the same lesson to my daughters."

This morning, that lesson means getting Cecilia and Yazbehl off to school. "Let's go," Ubel warns. "It's late."

"Will you be able to come to my swim meet today, Mama?" Yazbehl asks.

The girls are gathering books and lunches and getting a kiss good-bye. "I think so," Ubel replies. "But I can't make any promises. It will depend on how things go at the office."

"But I hope so," Ubel whispers to herself as she watches the girls walk off to school.

It's 8:15 A.M.: time to get to work. It takes Ubel about 30 minutes to drive to her office. Her office assistant, Nancy, is already at work.

Together, they review the day ahead. Ubel takes a deep breath: there's a lot to do today.

As Ubel heads to her desk, a man and a woman enter the office. "May we speak to Mrs. Velez?" the man asks. He speaks with a Spanish accent.

"Si, señor," Nancy replies. That's Spanish for "Yes, sir." Nancy can see that the couple is pleased that she speaks both languages. "Here's Mrs. Velez now," she says as Ubel turns to greet her first clients of the day.

Ubel smiles and leads the couple to her office. She can see that they are nervous, and she knows there must be some kind of trouble. The first thing she wants to do is put them both at ease. She asks them to sit down and assures them that everything they say will be kept secret. She speaks to them in Spanish. "Now," she asks, "what is the problem?"

"We want to become legal residents," the man explains. His name is Victor.

"Can you help us?" the woman asks. Her name is Maria.

"That depends on many things," Ubel replies. "Why don't you start at the beginning?"

Ubel has a good idea what the problem is. She practices a special kind of law. It is called immigration law, and it concerns the rights of people as they move from one country to another. Ubel helps people who want to immigrate, or move, to the United States.

She shakes her head as she listens. Ubel has heard the story before. She knows that there are tens of thousands of people like Victor and Maria who are living and working in the United States. They are called illegal residents. She has seen the worried looks before. She knows how hard life is for them: how lonely they are, far away from their families and their old way of life; how scared they are, scared that at any moment they will be forced to leave the new life they hope to build.

Ubel knows these new immigrants well. Many of them are Latinos, which means that they come from the Spanish-speaking countries of Central and South America. She knows their language. She knows their culture, or way of life. But she knows more than that. She understands their hopes and fears. She shares with them the pride of their Hispanic heritage. And she shares with them the dream of a "golden" future in America.

The man continues to speak. "We have been living here for three years now," he says. "We have heard that there is a new law that means we can live here legally. Is this true?" He looks at his wife. "We would like this very much." His wife nods her head in agreement. "Very much," she says.

Ubel has heard the story before. And she has seen the worried look before. But each case troubles her deeply. She is determined to do what she can to help, no matter how many times she hears the same story or sees the same look.

"Tell me the rest," Ubel says.

Victor takes a deep breath. "Several years ago," he begins, "we were living in a small town in Mexico." He tells his story in a quiet, nervous voice. "There was no work there for us. There was no way for us to get ahead. So we decided to go to the United States. Some of our friends had paid to have themselves smuggled across the border. They sold everything they owned to pay for the trip. It was a hard decision. We had to leave everything behind." The man pauses for a moment. Perhaps he is thinking about the village, and the family and friends there, he left behind.

Maria continues their story. "But we wanted to go. What choice did we really have? We couldn't stay in Mexico. That was no life for us. So we paid someone to bring us to the United States."

"We found a man to take us to Washington, D.C., where we have some relatives," Maria says. "We stayed there for a year. Then we moved to Wilmington. We heard that there was work here for . . . people like us."

The United States has often been called "a nation of immigrants." That's because so many people have come here from other countries. For much of our history, the United States government welcomed these immigrants to our country. In the 1700s and 1800s, millions of people immigrated to America.

They came for many reasons. Some came to escape the hardships of poverty and war. Some came to find a life of freedom and opportunity. But they all came to find a new home. America seemed to be a "golden land" to them.

But as the United States grew, more and more laws were passed to restrict or cut off immigration. In recent years, the government has not welcomed new immigrants. It has tried to stop them from entering the country.

Many new immigrants come from countries deep in poverty or torn apart by the bloodshed of civil war. Like so many immigrants before them, these people want a chance to start a new life in the "golden land" of America.

But unlike the men and women who came to the United States before them, these new immigrants must often enter the country illegally. They try to find whatever jobs they can. They live in fear and secrecy, afraid that the government will catch them and send them back to a life of poverty and hopelessness.

Listening to this story, Ubel is once again reminded of why she became a lawyer. For as long as she can remember, her dream was to be a lawyer. Because her father was a policeman, she grew up with a great respect for the law. She knew that certain rules were necessary in society just as they were in her home.

"We grew up with responsibilities at home," she recalls. "We helped with the meals, the shopping, and the housework. We grew up with rules, too. I understood that these rules were necessary so that we could live together happily as a family. When I was older and began to study the law, it was much the same idea. People everywhere need to know what is acceptable behavior and what is not so that they can live together peacefully."

But Ubel also learned that the law is about more than what is acceptable behavior and what is not. She learned from her parents that the law is also about helping people. It's about treating people fairly and equally.

"To give people a chance to make a better life for themselves: that is the most rewarding part of practicing law," Ubel says. "On the days when I am tired and frustrated, I think about people like Victor and Maria. They need someone who understands the law to look out for them. They need someone to make sure the law is on their side. I'm glad when that someone is me."

Ubel turns to Victor and Maria. "You are right about a new law," Ubel says to them. "The United States government has passed a law that gives illegal residents a chance to establish permanent residency. That means they can live and work here legally, without fear of being deported." Ubel explains the new law carefully: "The law allows some illegal residents to be granted amnesty, which means that they will not be punished for entering the country illegally. But not everyone qualifies for amnesty. I will do everything I can to help you, but first you must do something for me."

Ubel takes out a long form from her desk drawer. "I'm going to ask you some questions," she tells Victor and Maria. "The more information I have, the more I can help you." There are many questions to answer. When they have completed the form, Victor and Maria breathe a sigh of relief. They're glad that's over.

"But this is just the beginning of the process," Ubel reminds them. "There will be a hearing and even more paperwork at the Immigration Services Office. The officials there will decide if you can become permanent residents of the United States."

"But that's all for now," says Ubel. Maria turns to Ubel with a questioning look.

"Yes?" Ubel says.

Maria asks: "Do you think we have a chance?"

"I think you have a good chance," Ubel answers.

"Muchas gracias," Maria says, with a newfound smile.

Ubel replies with a smile of her own. "De nada," she says. She watches Victor and Maria leave the office.

As Ubel returns to her paperwork, she is hopeful that she can help Victor and Maria. But she can't help thinking how many people there are like them.

And she can't help thinking how much work there is
to do. Ubel spends the next several hours filling out legal
documents and government forms. Many people think that
lawyers spend most of their time arguing exciting cases in
crowded courtrooms. That's the way it looks on television.

You may know how a trial works. A trial occurs when someone has been accused of a crime. The person who has been accused is called the defendant. The defendant's lawyer is called the defense attorney. The defense attorney tries to prove that the defendant is innocent, which means that he or she didn't commit the crime. Another lawyer, called the prosecutor, tries to prove that the defendant is guilty, that he or she did commit the crime. The defense attorney and the prosecutor call different people to testify, or tell what they know about the crime. They ask tough questions while the jury listens carefully. The jury are the men and women who decide whether someone is guilty.

But it's not always the way it looks on television. For most lawyers, sitting behind a desk piled high with legal forms is a more familiar scene. "I love my job," Ubel says, "but sometimes I feel like I'm drowning in paperwork."

It's 12:30 P.M.: time to take a break from the paperwork and get a bite to eat. Ubel walks briskly to the corner of Market and High streets, where she orders a hot dog from a streetcart vendor.

"With extra mustard," she says.

Ubel leans against the gray stone wall of the nearby building. It's a building she knows well. This is the county courthouse. It's here that Ubel represents many of her clients. In fact, she has to argue a case here tomorrow morning. She watches as other lawyers, judges, district attorneys, and court clerks come out to take a break and get a breath of fresh air.

Suddenly, she hears a voice call her name. "Mrs. Velez," someone calls from the direction of the courthouse. Ubel sees a young woman walking toward her. Her name is Sandra. She's a new member of Ubel's support group. A support group is a group of people who share a similar problem. They get together to talk and to share ideas. They try to help each other.

Ubel's support group is made up of women who work in the legal profession. They are lawyers, judges, legal assistants, and office managers. Most of them are working moms. "It isn't easy," Ubel says, "to be a good mother and wife and to meet the challenges of such a demanding career. Working moms often feel that they have to be everywhere at once. And, of course, that's just not possible."

That's why Ubel helped to form this support group. "It's important to discuss the problems we face at home and on the job. It isn't easy for any of us, but sometimes it helps to know that you're not the only one trying to manage a very complicated life."

Sandra came to the support group for the first time last week. "Did you enjoy the discussion?" Ubel asks.

"Oh, it was great," Sandra says. "I thought I was the only lawyer in town who was trying to prepare cases for court and raise children, too. What a relief to find out that I wasn't alone!"

Ubel knows exactly what Sandra means. As Sandra hurries back to work, Ubel remembers how difficult it was when *she* first became a working mom.

When Ubel graduated from college, she knew just what she wanted to do next. She had been dreaming about it for a long time. She applied to the University of Puerto Rico Law School. Even now, Ubel can remember how she felt when she found out that she had been accepted to the law school. "All my hard work really paid off," she recalls. "I was a step away from my dream of being a lawyer."

It may have been only one step, but it was a big one. Law school means three years of hard work. "The law courses were very demanding," Ubel says, looking back on many long days and nights of studying. "It was a hectic time for me and Manuel. And that was *before* the baby!"

One week after Ubel finished law school, she gave birth to her first daughter, Yazbehl. "Now, it was a *very* hectic time! But a happy one, too. We were delighted to be the parents of a beautiful little girl. It was all so new to us. And so much work!"

While taking care of her new baby, Ubel was also studying for the "bar." This is the final test that law students must pass in order to become professional lawyers. Ubel needed to study as much as possible, but many nights Yazbehl wouldn't go to sleep. So Ubel read to her newborn daughter from the law books she was studying. "Of course, Yazbehl didn't understand a word I was saying. But it didn't seem to matter as long as I read in a soothing tone. I decided that storybooks could wait until I passed the bar."

Ubel did pass the bar. Her lifelong dream of becoming a lawyer was true at last!

Her family was growing, too. Soon there was another little one to take care of. And, then, when Cecilia was only five months old, Manuel was offered a new job in the United States.

"It was a big change for the Velez family," Ubel says. "We were so excited about coming to live in the United States. Of course, Puerto Rico is a territory of the United States, but the language and culture are quite different. We left behind the places we knew and the people we loved. We left our old life 2,000 miles away."

Ubel wanted to find a job where she could use her legal skills to provide a service to the Hispanic community. Just a few weeks after moving to Wilmington, she found what she wanted. She was hired to work for La Comunidad Hispana, a group that provides housing and immigration assistance to the Hispanic community.

It was a perfect job, but it meant that Ubel would have to find a full-time baby sitter for her two small daughters. Fortunately, a neighbor who was also from Puerto Rico agreed to watch the girls.

"I knew her well," says Ubel, "and I trusted her completely with the care of Yazbehl and Cecilia. She was like a second mother to them."

Ubel looks at her watch. It's 1:15 P.M.: time to get back to work. This afternoon, Ubel has to be at the Immigration Services Office in Lima, Pennsylvania. There she will help new Hispanic immigrants who are applying for residency. The immigration office is about 30 minutes away.

Ubel makes a quick stop back at her office to finish some last-minute details and to pick up her messages. One of the phone messages is from Manuel. "See you at the swim meet?" it reads. "I'm going to try," Ubel thinks, as she gathers several folders bulging with legal forms and documents that she needs for the afternoon.

Ubel spends the rest of the day at the Immigration Services Office. She helps each immigrant through the application process. It's a good thing she can speak both Spanish and English. Many of the new immigrants speak only Spanish. So Ubel reviews the written applications with an immigration officer to make sure everything is in order.

It's 4:30 P.M.: time to get back in the car and drive to her daughter's swim meet. There will be just enough time.

Forty minutes later, Ubel is sitting on the outdoor bleachers next to Manuel. The score is tied going into the last race. The last race is a relay, and Yazbehl swims the third leg for her team, the Tigers. Everyone is up and cheering as the fourth and final swimmers sprint to the finish. It's going to be close. But the Tigers win!

"I'm so glad you're here," Yazbehl tells her parents as they give her a big victory hug.

"Hey, you're wet," Manuel notices, as everyone laughs.

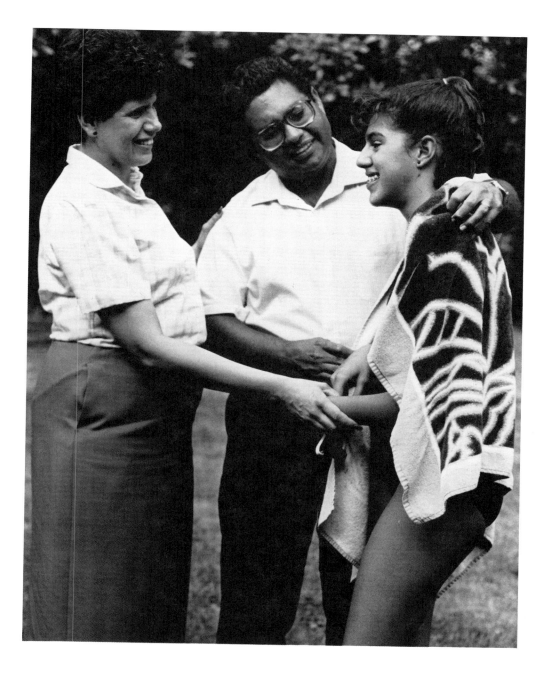

It's 7:00 P.M.: time for a quiet dinner. Everyone is hungry, and the beef stew disappears quickly.

"Did anything interesting happen at school today, Cecilia?" Ubel asks her younger daughter.

"Not really," Cecilia answers. "But I have a big math test tomorrow," she says. "Could you help me study tonight?"

"Of course," Ubel replies. "While we do the dishes, you get everything ready."

"And how's your book report coming along?" Manuel asks Yazbehl.

"I've finished the outline."

"Well, let's take a look," he says.

As the girls race off to get their homework, Ubel and Manuel clean up the kitchen. "I got a letter from my mother today," Ubel says. "She's so happy that we're coming to Puerto Rico for a visit."

"So am I," Manuel replies. "We can use a break."

"Only a month away," says Ubel.

Ubel and Manuel spend time going over the girls' schoolwork. There are also household chores that need to be done: clothes to wash, bills to pay, trash to take out, and a hundred other things to do. "It seems that our nights are just as busy as our days," Ubel says.

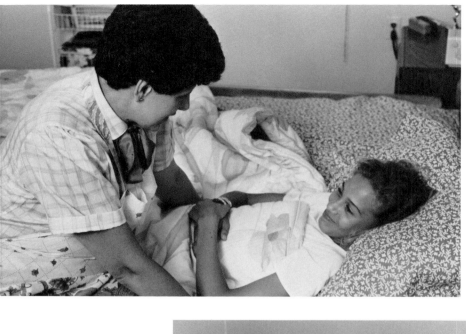

But before it's "lights out" for Yazbehl and Cecilia, Ubel pays each girl a special visit. "The days are so busy that I don't really get a chance to talk with my daughters," Ubel says. "So I set aside this time to be with them, to talk with them. Most of all, I set aside time just to listen to them."

It's 10:00 P.M.: time for Ubel and Manuel to enjoy a few quiet minutes together. They fold the laundry as they watch the evening news. One of the news stories is about several new immigration laws. Ubel wonders how these laws will affect her clients.

"It sounds like another busy year for you," Manuel says to his wife.

Ubel nods in agreement. "Yes, another busy year," she thinks as she takes a few moments to read before going to bed. "And another busy day tomorrow."

She leans back against the pillows at the end of the bed. Closing her eyes, she tries to picture the county courtroom tomorrow morning. She tries to picture herself standing before the judge and jury, arguing her case.

But her mind has other ideas. Instead of standing before a judge and jury, she is sitting on a white, sandy beach bordered by palm trees. It's the beach near her mother's home in Puerto Rico.

"Only a month away," she thinks.

Glossary

amnesty	when a government forgives a person for a crime
bar	the final test a person must pass to become a lawyer
client	a person whom a lawyer helps
court	the place where a trial is held
defendant	a person accused of breaking the law
defense lawyer	a lawyer who tries to prove that a defendant is not guilty
deported	when people are sent back to the country they came from
Hispanic	a person of Spanish or Latin American origin
illegal resident	a person from one country who lives in another country without permission
immigrant	a person who moves from one country to another
immigration	the movement of a person from one country to another
immigration law	the area of law that concerns the rights of people as they move from one country to another
jury	the people who decide whether someone is guilty
law	a government's rule about what people are allowed to do
lawyer	a person who gives advice to people about the law
prosecutor	a lawyer who tries to prove that a defendant is guilty
support group	people with a similar problem who meet to share ideas
trial	a procedure to determine if a person has broken the law